PLANET UNDER PRESSURE
CLIMATE CHANGE

Mike Unwin

www.raintreepublishers.co.uk

Visit our website to find out more information about **Raintree** books.

To order:

☎ Phone 44 (0) 1865 888112

🖹 Send a fax to 44 (0) 1865 314091

💻 Visit the Raintree bookshop at **www.raintreepublishers.co.uk**
to browse our catalogue and order online.

MONKEY PUZZLE MEDIA LTD

Produced for Raintree by
Monkey Puzzle Media Ltd
Gissing's Farm, Fressingfield
Suffolk IP21 5SH, UK

First published in Great Britain by Raintree,
Halley Court, Jordan Hill, Oxford OX2 8EJ,
part of Harcourt Education.
Raintree is a registered trademark
of Harcourt Education Ltd.

Editorial: Clare Weaver
Design: Jane Hawkins
Picture Research: Laura Barwick
Production: Chloe Bloom

Originated by Dot Gradations
Printed and bound in China by South China
Printing Company

10 digit ISBN 1 4062 0536 2
13 digit ISBN 978 1 4062 0536 7
11 10 09 08 07
10 9 8 7 6 5 4 3 2 1

**British Library Cataloguing in
Publication Data**
Unwin, Mike
Climate change. – (Planet under pressure)
1.Climatic changes – Juvenile literature
2.Climatic changes – Environmental aspects –
Juvenile literature
I.Title
363.7'3874

Acknowledgements
Alamy p. **28** (Ashley Cooper); Gary Braasch p. **15**;
Corbis p. **9** (Phil Schermeister); FLPA p. **11** (Frans
Lanting/Minden Pictures); Fogden Photos p. **31**;
Getty Images pp. **6** (Art Wolfe/Image Bank), **7**
(Mark Mawson), **12**, **16** (Sakis Papadopoulos/
Image Bank), **19**, **24** (AFP), **26** (AFP), **27** (National
Geographic), **30** (National Geographic), **32** (Image
Bank), **33** (AFP), **36**, **38** (AFP), **39** (Jim Cummins/
Taxi), **41**; Nature Picture Library p. **20** (Lynn M.
Stone); NHPA p. **21** (Guy Edwardes); Science
Photo Library p. **25** (Sinclair Stammers); Still
Pictures pp. **10** (Mark Edwards), **23** (Charlotte
Thege), **29** (John Maier), **35** (Hartmut Schwarzbach),
37 (Charlotte Thege), **40** (Martin Bond). Maps
and graphs by Martin Darlison at Encompass
Graphics.

Cover photograph of dead trees reproduced with
permission of MPM Images (Corbis Digital Stock)
and of flooding in Bangladesh with permission
of Panos Pictures (G.M.B. Akash).

Every effort has been made to contact copyright
holders of any material reproduced in this book.
Any omissions will be rectified in subsequent
printings if notice is given to the publishers.

Disclaimer
All the Internet addresses (URLs) given in this
book were valid at the time of going to press.
However, due to the dynamic nature of the
Internet, some addresses may have changed, or
sites may have changed or ceased to exist since
publication. While the author and publishers
regret any inconvenience this may cause readers,
no responsibility for any such changes can be
accepted by either the author or the publishers.

Contents

Any words appearing in the text in bold, like this, are explained in the Glossary.

Climate change around the world

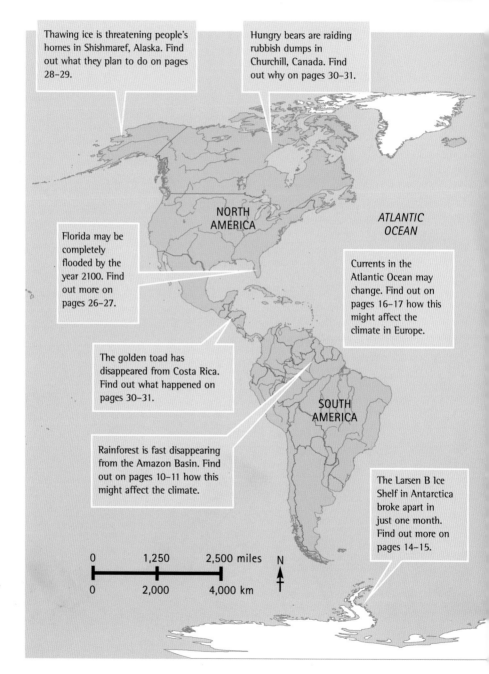

Thawing ice is threatening people's homes in Shishmaref, Alaska. Find out what they plan to do on pages 28–29.

Hungry bears are raiding rubbish dumps in Churchill, Canada. Find out why on pages 30–31.

Florida may be completely flooded by the year 2100. Find out more on pages 26–27.

Currents in the Atlantic Ocean may change. Find out on pages 16–17 how this might affect the climate in Europe.

The golden toad has disappeared from Costa Rica. Find out what happened on pages 30–31.

Rainforest is fast disappearing from the Amazon Basin. Find out on pages 10–11 how this might affect the climate.

The Larsen B Ice Shelf in Antarctica broke apart in just one month. Find out more on pages 14–15.

NORTH AMERICA

ATLANTIC OCEAN

SOUTH AMERICA

0   1,250   2,500 miles

0   2,000   4,000 km

N

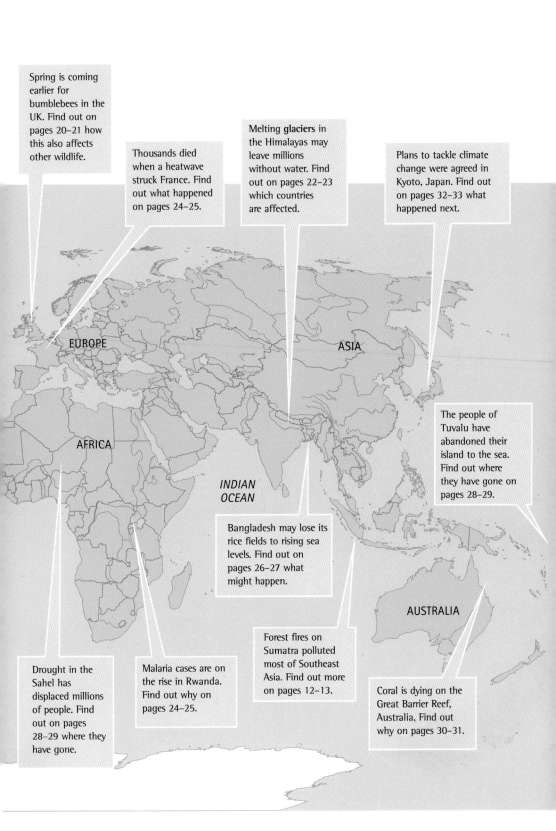

Spring is coming earlier for bumblebees in the UK. Find out on pages 20–21 how this also affects other wildlife.

Thousands died when a heatwave struck France. Find out what happened on pages 24–25.

Melting **glaciers** in the Himalayas may leave millions without water. Find out on pages 22–23 which countries are affected.

Plans to tackle climate change were agreed in Kyoto, Japan. Find out on pages 32–33 what happened next.

EUROPE

ASIA

AFRICA

INDIAN OCEAN

The people of Tuvalu have abandoned their island to the sea. Find out where they have gone on pages 28–29.

Bangladesh may lose its rice fields to rising sea levels. Find out on pages 26–27 what might happen.

AUSTRALIA

Drought in the Sahel has displaced millions of people. Find out on pages 28–29 where they have gone.

Malaria cases are on the rise in Rwanda. Find out why on pages 24–25.

Forest fires on Sumatra polluted most of Southeast Asia. Find out more on pages 12–13.

Coral is dying on the Great Barrier Reef, Australia. Find out why on pages 30–31.

A warmer world

Our climate is changing. Average temperatures around the world rose by 0.6°C (1°F) during the 20th century, with the 1990s being the warmest decade since records began in 1772. This change is known as global warming and it shows no sign of stopping. Scientists believe that temperatures may increase by up to 5.8°C (10°F) by the year 2100.

TIPPING THE BALANCE

A rise of 0.6°C (1°F) may not sound like much; you would probably not even notice it in your bathwater. But Earth's climate is delicately balanced and small changes can have big effects. At the end of the last **ice age**, 11,000 years ago, the climate was only about 5°C (9°F) colder than today. Today's global warming is already having a big impact, causing melting ice caps, rising sea levels, storms, droughts, and floods. This is affecting all life on Earth, including people.

WHAT IS CLIMATE CHANGE?

The climate is the typical pattern of weather that any particular place experiences. For instance, the UK or Oregon in the United States have warm summers and mild winters, with rainfall all year round; it rarely gets very hot or very cold. The Sahara Desert, in Africa, by contrast, is very hot for much of the year and has very little rainfall. The pattern stays roughly the same in each part of the world from one year to the next – even from one century to the next – so that the people living there know what to expect. Climate change is when these patterns start to alter.

Scientists think that erupting volcanoes may have affected Earth's climate in the past.

HISTORY OF CHANGE

Climate change is nothing new. Fossils beneath the ice show that 90 million years ago **deciduous** forests grew in the Arctic and dinosaurs roamed the Antarctic, proving that conditions were once much warmer there. Scientists have suggested many reasons for this, including shifts in the pattern of Earth's **orbit** that affect how much warmth reaches us from the Sun. Major periods of volcanic eruptions, that choke the air with dust and gases, can also have an effect.

However, past changes mostly took place very slowly, over thousands – or even millions – of years. For the last few thousand years the climate has been relatively stable, which is why people have been able to settle all around the globe. Today things are changing: temperatures are at their highest for thousands of years and the warming is picking up speed.

WHO IS TO BLAME?

Most scientists believe that people are largely responsible for today's climate change. They think that the way we live, especially the way we burn fuels for energy, is increasing global warming. Unless we change our ways, say these scientists, Earth may be heading towards disaster. Some scientists, however, believe that global warming is part of a natural cycle and that people have nothing to do with it. Either way, the world is definitely heating up and problems lie ahead.

Global warming today is turning parts of Earth into deserts, where livestock can't survive.

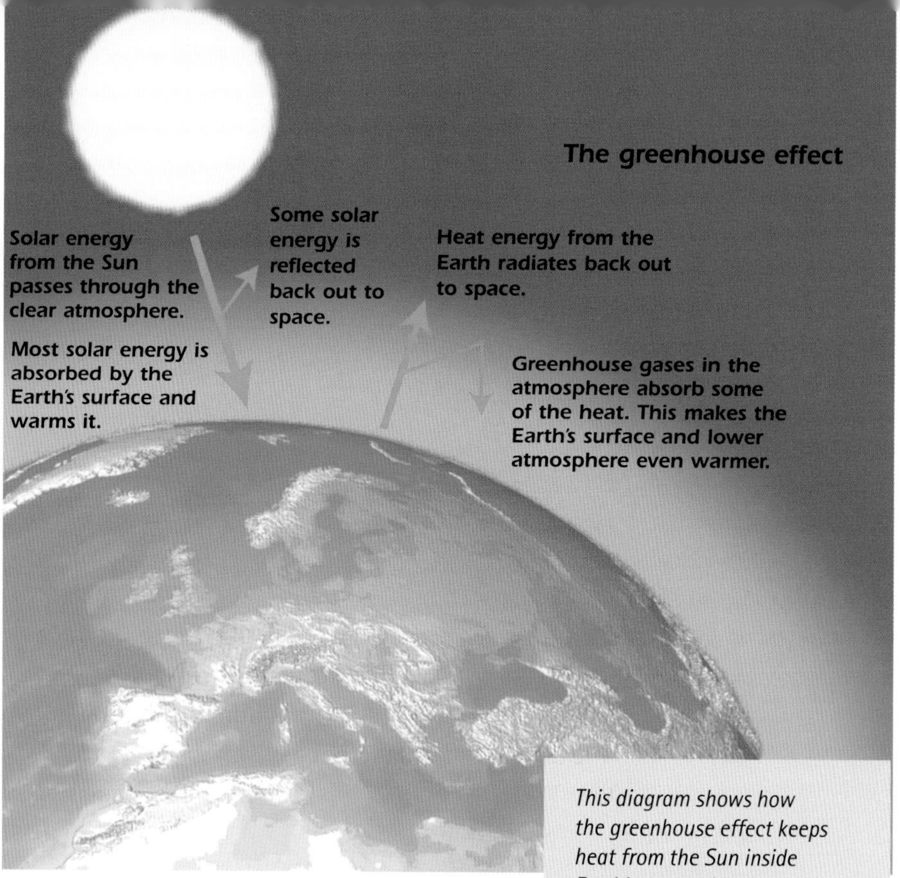

Solar energy
from the Sun
passes through the
clear atmosphere.

Some solar
energy is
reflected
back out to
space.

Heat energy from the
Earth radiates back out
to space.

Most solar energy is
absorbed by the
Earth's surface and
warms it.

Greenhouse gases in the
atmosphere absorb some
of the heat. This makes the
Earth's surface and lower
atmosphere even warmer.

*This diagram shows how
the greenhouse effect keeps
heat from the Sun inside
Earth's atmosphere.*

Living in a greenhouse

The Earth stays warm because of something called the "greenhouse effect".
This is a natural process, in which gases in Earth's **atmosphere**, known as
greenhouse gases, trap heat from the Sun – just like the glass walls of a
greenhouse do. The greenhouse effect is essential to all life. Without it,
Earth's surface temperature would plunge to −18°C (−0.4°F), making Earth
much too cold for anything to live on.

ENERGY TRAP

Sunlight supplies Earth with energy, called solar energy. About half the
sunlight that reaches Earth is reflected back into space by snow and ice on
the surface or dust in the atmosphere. The rest is absorbed on Earth's
surface where it is turned into heat. This heat radiates upwards. Some of it
escapes back into space, but clouds of **water vapour** and greenhouse gases
trap the rest of it in the atmosphere. Here it remains, providing energy to
keep life going on Earth's surface below.

CARBON DIOXIDE

Several different greenhouse gases occur naturally in the atmosphere. Carbon dioxide (CO_2) is the most important, because there is so much of it. It is produced by plants, which release it into the atmosphere when they rot or burn. Green plants reabsorb some CO_2 to use in **photosynthesis** – the process by which they make food from sunlight. Some CO_2 also dissolves in the oceans. The rest remains in the atmosphere.

OTHER GREENHOUSE GASES

Other greenhouse gases occur in smaller quantities. Methane (CH_4) is produced when vegetation rots or burns without the presence of oxygen. It is 21 times more effective than CO_2 at absorbing heat. Rubbish dumps and rice fields generate methane – as do grazing animals, which produce it during digestion and release it into the air. Nitrous oxide (N_2O) is released when farmers use chemical fertilizers and manure on the soil. Other greenhouse gases include human-made compounds called chlorofluorocarbons (CFCs). These were once found in appliances such as fridges – though they are seldom used today.

UPSETTING THE BALANCE

The greenhouse effect has worked perfectly for thousands of years. It keeps Earth's climate steady, by balancing the amount of energy entering the atmosphere with the amount leaving it. Plants and oceans ensure that there are just enough – but not too many – greenhouse gases in the atmosphere. However, any change can upset the balance. That is what seems to be happening today.

Grazing cattle and other livestock produce large amounts of the greenhouse gas methane.

Choking the atmosphere

The amount of carbon dioxide in Earth's atmosphere has risen by 31 per cent over the last 250 years and each year it is rising faster. At this rate, scientists expect it to double by the end of the 21st century. Most scientists now believe that people have played an important part in this increase. In the 1990s, we released almost 7 billion tonnes (8 billion tons) of CO_2 each year; this is expected to rise to 9.8 billion tonnes (11 billion tons) by 2020.

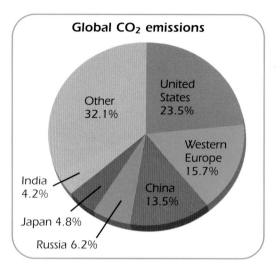

Global CO₂ emissions

- Other 32.1%
- United States 23.5%
- Western Europe 15.7%
- China 13.5%
- Russia 6.2%
- Japan 4.8%
- India 4.2%

THE AGE OF MACHINES

Ever since the **Industrial Revolution**, when **developed countries** first began to rely on machines, people have been using an increasing amount of fossil fuels. Fossil fuels are natural deposits, such as coal, oil, and natural gas that formed when dead plants became buried underground millions of years ago. They are full of the carbon that the plants absorbed when alive. Burning them releases CO_2 into the atmosphere.

Power stations burn huge quantities of fossil fuel, releasing huge amounts of carbon dioxide into the atmosphere.

Today, fossil fuels provide almost 75 per cent of global energy. Modern life in wealthier countries is hard to imagine without them: they drive our vehicles, power our factories, produce our electricity, heat our homes, and manufacture all sorts of products. Fossil fuels are now being used up 100,000 times faster than they formed.

TIMBER!

In the last 200 years we have also chopped down nearly half the world's forests in order to provide timber or clear land for farming. Tropical rainforests have suffered the most: an area of tropical forest the size of two football pitches is lost around the world every second. Chopping down and burning trees releases huge amounts of CO_2. With fewer trees left to absorb it, more builds up as greenhouse gases in the atmosphere.

The tarsier of Southeast Asia is one of the many animals whose home is threatened as rainforests disappear.

OTHER GREENHOUSE GASES

People are also pumping more of other greenhouse gases into the atmosphere. The amount of waste that we now dump in **landfill sites**, and the increase in livestock and rice fields to feed our growing population, have caused methane levels to soar. Nitrous oxide emissions have also risen, due to all the chemical fertilizers and manure that farmers use.

AROUND THE WORLD

Not every part of the world produces CO_2 at the same rate. Developed countries, such as Europe and North America, produce far more per person than **developing countries**, such as those in Africa. For instance, the average US family uses as much fossil fuel in two days as the average Tanzanian family does in a whole year. However, when greenhouse gases build up in the atmosphere they affect the climate everywhere.

Our climate today

You do not have to travel far to spot signs of global warming. Some parts of the world are warming faster than others, though warming in one place can affect another on the other side of the globe.

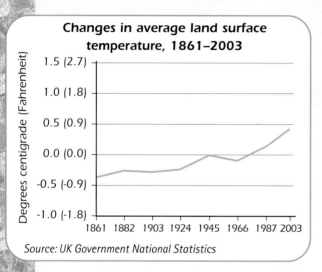

Changes in average land surface temperature, 1861–2003

Degrees centigrade (Fahrenheit)

1.5 (2.7)
1.0 (1.8)
0.5 (0.9)
0.0 (0.0)
-0.5 (-0.9)
-1.0 (-1.8)

1861 1882 1903 1924 1945 1966 1987 2003

Source: UK Government National Statistics

SUMMER SWELTER

For simple evidence of global warming, just check the rising thermometer. In central England, for instance, four of the five warmest years since records began have occurred since 1990, with August 2003 recording a highest-ever temperature of 38.5°C (101°F). Extreme heat usually occurs inland, far from the cooling effects of the sea. Recent summers have brought deadly heatwaves to Chicago, in central United States, and Andhra Pradesh, in central India. A heatwave struck central Europe in 2003, with temperatures 8°C (15°F) higher than usual. An estimated 35,000 people died.

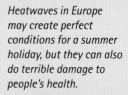

Heatwaves in Europe may create perfect conditions for a summer holiday, but they can also do terrible damage to people's health.

DRYING OUT

Long hot periods without rain can cause droughts, when the land dries up and there is not enough water to go round. In parts of the Sahel region of northern Africa, the amount of rainfall has virtually halved since the 1960s. Meanwhile, southern Africa has lost one-fifth of its rainfall since 1950. Both these regions look set to get even drier. Scientists suspect the reason may lie in changing ocean currents triggered by the effects of global warming, especially at the North and South Poles.

UP IN SMOKE

Hot, dry summer weather creates perfect conditions for forest fires. The soil dries out and dead leaves on the forest floor burn very easily. There is also little rain to damp down the fires. Since 1980, Canada has lost an average of 2.4 million hectares (6 million acres) of forest to fires each year, an area larger than Israel or the US state of New Hampshire. This is more than double the amount lost in the previous 30 years. It is no coincidence that Canada's hottest years and longest droughts have occurred during this time.

FOREST FIRE FEEDBACK

Not only does global warming help cause forest fires: forest fires may, in turn, help cause global warming. This is called a "positive feedback loop". The fires release CO_2 into the atmosphere, which boosts global warming. This dries vegetation and results in more fires, which boosts global warming even more – and so it goes on. In 1997–1998 the concentration of CO_2 in the atmosphere rose even higher than scientists had predicted. Much had come from Southeast Asia, where enormous forest fires on the Indonesian island of Sumatra blackened the skies for months on end.

WHAT DO YOU THINK?
We can stop global warming by planting more trees

- Trees absorb CO_2 from the atmosphere, which helps reduce global warming.
- But trees add large amounts of CO_2 to the atmosphere when they burn, so forest fires speed up global warming.

Meltdown

Global warming is happening faster in the **polar regions** than anywhere else. Since 1940, the average temperature has risen by 1°C (3°F) in the Arctic and an amazing 2.5°C (4°F) in the Antarctic. Today, the Earth's big freezer is starting to defrost.

SHRINKING ICE

Antarctica is the coldest place on Earth. Ice sheets cover the land and a layer of sea ice twice as big as the United States forms around the coast each winter. Global warming is causing the sea ice to shrink and the ice sheets on land to start melting. Less sea ice means less of the Sun's energy is reflected back into space, leaving the oceans more likely to warm up. Warmer water absorbs less CO_2, so more builds up in the atmosphere and increases global warming. This is another positive feedback loop.

Breaking up

In 1992, a section of the Larsen Ice Shelf broke away from the Antarctic Peninsula. About 3,250 km² (1,254 sq miles) – an area larger than London, UK, or Rhode Island, USA – disintegrated in just 35 days, splitting into thousands of icebergs that drifted out to sea. The ice shelf was about 220 m (722 ft) thick and had probably existed since the last ice age. It was one of five in Antarctica that together have shrunk by nearly 13,500 km² (5,212 sq miles) since 1974. "It is hard to believe that 500 billion tonnes (550 billion tons) of ice sheet has disintegrated in less than a month," said Dr David Vaughan of the British Antarctic Survey.

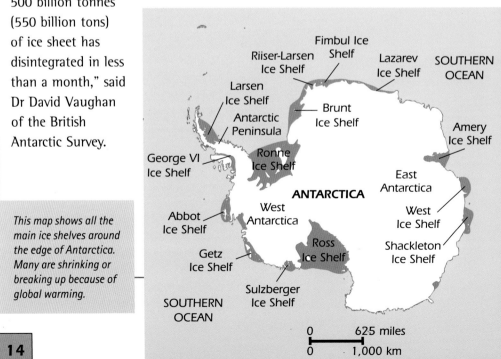

This map shows all the main ice shelves around the edge of Antarctica. Many are shrinking or breaking up because of global warming.

Meanwhile, disappearing sea ice is leaving Arctic coastlines at the mercy of storms. The Arctic ground is also starting to thaw, causing landslides and **erosion**. Methane that had been trapped in the frozen soil for 10,000 years is escaping into the atmosphere. This increases the level of greenhouse gases and makes the problem even worse.

ICE RIVERS

About 6 per cent of the world's ice is locked up in **glaciers** – the frozen rivers of ice found in high **latitudes** and mountain ranges. Most of Earth's 160,000 glaciers are now melting and shrinking. Mount Kilimanjaro in East Africa has lost three-quarters of its ice between 1900 and 2000. As glaciers shrink, the rivers below them have less water to carry to the lowlands.

LEARNING FROM ICE

The top picture of Pasterze Glacier in Austria was taken in 1875. The bottom picture was taken from the same place in 2004, showing just how much ice has melted.

The polar regions help scientists to find out more about climate change. Ice extracted from deep within ice sheets, called core samples, contains particles of dust and bubbles of atmospheric gases preserved thousands of years ago. These reveal prehistoric climate patterns and suggest what we might expect in the future. Changes that scientists observe at the Poles can alert us to global warming elsewhere.

Sea change

Scientists are noticing changes at sea that may also be connected to global warming. For the first time in human history, sea level has begun to rise fast enough to measure. Ocean currents, meanwhile, are also beginning to change.

CREEPING UP

Sea levels have always changed. During the height of the last ice age, 21,000 years ago, they were 135 m (443 ft) lower than today, leaving a bridge of land between Asia and North America. But today, the sea is rising faster than at any time for 5,000 years. In the last two decades it has advanced by about 2 mm (0.07 in) per year. Some experts predict it may rise by up to 88 cm (35 in) by the year 2100. This may not sound much, but it is enough to flood 36,000 km^2 (13,900 sq miles) of land (an area larger than Belgium or the state of Maryland, US) in the United States alone.

TOP-UPS AND EXPANSION

As glaciers and ice sheets melt, the fresh water that was trapped inside them flows off the land and tops up the oceans. It is replaced by water that **evaporates** from the oceans and falls back on land as snow. This makes sure that sea levels do not change, but scientists think that global warming may soon cause more ice to melt than can be replaced by snowfall. This would add water to the oceans and cause sea levels to rise.

Meanwhile, there is another more important cause of rising sea levels. As the world gets warmer, so do the oceans. When sea water is heated it expands and its **density** decreases. This is called thermal expansion.

It means that the water takes up a greater volume of space and so pushes up the sea level. We may not be able to see thermal expansion happening, but scientists believe it will be the main cause of sea-level rise over the 21st century.

POLAR PROBLEMS

Scientists are not yet sure how much the warming of the Arctic and Antarctic will affect global sea levels. Melting sea ice adds no extra water to the oceans, since when floating ice melts, it only replaces the volume of water that it originally displaced. But ice melting on land is different. Antarctica is covered by an ice sheet that is, on average, 2.5 km (1.5 miles) thick, and about 4.8 km (3 miles) at its thickest. Scientists are worried that one part of this, the huge Western Antarctic Ice Sheet, could one day collapse completely. This would cause a sea rise of at least 6 m (20 ft). They do not think this will happen for at least a thousand years, but there are already signs of disintegration around the edges.

CURRENT CONCERNS

Ocean currents work like conveyor belts. Warm currents flow north and south from the tropical regions at the Equator, then cool down when they reach the polar seas. Cold water is denser than warm water, so it sinks to the bottom and travels slowly back towards the tropics. This conveyor system helps transport warm water from the Caribbean to Western Europe and prevents it from becoming too cold. But some scientists worry that global warming may change things. Higher sea surface temperatures and melting ice from glaciers would prevent the salt water from becoming too cold or dense enough to sink.

The North Atlantic conveyor would come to a halt. The warm current, known as the Gulf Stream, would no longer reach European shores and life in countries such as the United Kingdom would become much colder.

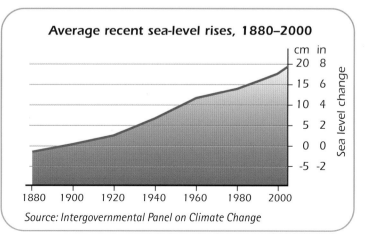

Average recent sea-level rises, 1880–2000

Source: Intergovernmental Panel on Climate Change

Stormy skies

The world's weather seems to be taking a turn for the worse, with **hurricanes**, heatwaves, floods, and other extreme events all becoming more common in many areas. In 1998, Hurricane Mitch wreaked havoc in Central America. In 1999, Bangladesh and Venezuela both suffered some of their worst floods ever. In 2002, record floods and heatwaves left Europe reeling. Some scientists believe that all these events offer further evidence of global warming.

BREWING UP A STORM

As the ocean's surface warms up, more water evaporates and increases the energy in the atmosphere. This produces more winds, rain, and violent weather. Since the 1950s, the number of severe tropical storms has increased in many parts of the world. This has coincided with a steady rise in average sea surface temperatures, especially in the **tropics**, where today they are more than 1°C (3°F) warmer than a century ago. A hurricane needs a surface temperature of 27°C (80°F) in order to get going. Once started, it needs only warm water to help it build up strength and speed.

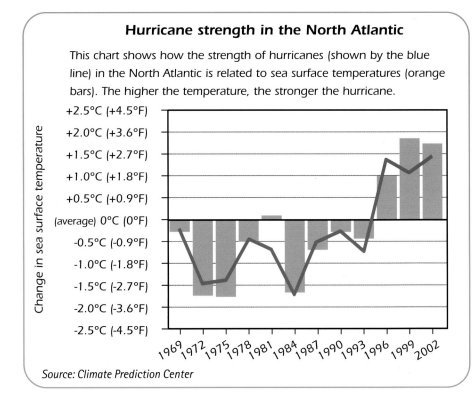

Hurricane strength in the North Atlantic

This chart shows how the strength of hurricanes (shown by the blue line) in the North Atlantic is related to sea surface temperatures (orange bars). The higher the temperature, the stronger the hurricane.

Change in sea surface temperature

Source: Climate Prediction Center

Hurricane Katrina

The Atlantic hurricane season affects the southern and eastern United States every year between June and November. An average season produces ten tropical storms, of which six become hurricanes. But, in recent seasons, the hurricanes have become stronger and more frequent. 2005 was the most active season ever recorded, with 26 tropical storms and 14 hurricanes. One of these – Hurricane Katrina – turned out to be the most destructive in US history. Katrina struck the Louisiana coast on 29 August. It devastated an area of 233,000 km^2 (90,000 sq miles), almost as large as the United Kingdom, and completely flooded New Orleans. At least 1,350 people died, over one million were displaced and an estimated five million people lost their power supplies.

Rescue workers had to use boats to get around New Orleans after Hurricane Katrina struck in 2005.

WHO KNOWS?

Scientists cannot yet say for certain what is making our weather more violent. There have been busy hurricane periods in the past, such as during the 1920s, so the recent increase in hurricanes may be part of a natural cycle. But they cannot rule out climate change as a possible cause, or dismiss the role that people play in global warming. We do know that as Hurricane Katrina passed over the Gulf of Mexico in August 2005, the surface waters were about 2°C (4°F) warmer than normal for the time of year. Whatever the explanation, scientists agree that more of the same lies ahead.

WHAT DO YOU THINK? Whose fault was Hurricane Katrina?

- Some people think that global warming caused by human activities was responsible for Hurricane Katrina.
- Others think that Hurricane Katrina was just a natural tragedy that nobody could do anything about.

Trees are now growing in parts of the Arctic where they have never been seen before.

Nature on the move

Climate change affects nature, too. Global warming alters **habitats**, causing plants and animals to disappear from some places, or to show up where they have never been before. Animal behaviour patterns are also changing, with some species travelling further or breeding earlier than before.

NORTHERN GREENING

Warmer conditions in the Arctic are allowing pine and birch forests to spread northwards into **tundra** areas, where the land was once too cold for trees to grow. This spread, known as "northern greening", has seen forests in places such as Russia and Canada advance by an amazing 150–540 km (93–335 miles) between 1900 and 2000. Some animals benefit from the change, while others lose out. For instance, the North American red fox is spreading northwards and becoming more widespread, but this is at the expense of its cousin, the Arctic fox, whose tundra home is shrinking.

ALL AT SEA

Marine wildlife is on the move as the oceans heat up. In recent years, fishermen have been astonished to catch tropical fish, such as rainbow wrasse, and anchovies in the once chilly waters of the North Sea. These changes also affect other wildlife. For instance, marine creatures, such as squid and **plankton**, are declining off the west coast of the United States as the water there becomes too warm for them. As a result, California's population of sooty shearwaters – a seabird that feeds on these creatures – fell by 90 per cent between 1987 and 1993.

BLOOMING EARLY

Milder winters mean an earlier spring. In Europe and North America nature is getting going in a hurry.
- Cherry trees in Washington, DC now reach peak bloom on 3 April. Before 1970, the average date was 5 April.

- Bumblebees in the UK usually emerge in February. Since 1993, there have been many January sightings, with the earliest being on 23 December 2003.
- **Marmots** in the Rocky Mountains are emerging from **hibernation** on average 23 days earlier than they did 23 years ago.
- European frogs are **spawning** on average nine to ten days earlier.

Changing ranges

Plants and animals all around the world are finding new homes, as a warmer climate allows them to live in places that were once too cold.

Where	Animal/plant	What's happening?
Europe	Butterflies	22 butterfly species spread northwards by 35–240 km (22–150 miles) over the last century
Austrian Alps	Alpine plants	Alpine plants moved higher up mountain slopes over a 70–90 year period
Banks Island, Canada	Birds	Birds common further south, such as robins and barn swallows, are appearing for the first time
Monterey Bay, California	Shoreline sea life	Invertebrates such as limpets, snails, and sea stars spread northwards between 1931 and 1994
Argentine Islands	Antarctic flowering plants	The Antarctic pearlwort and the Antarctic hairgrass spread rapidly between 1964 and 1990

All change for UK birds

The United Kingdom is one of the many countries where warmer weather is changing the kinds of birds you can expect to see. Some are becoming scarcer as climate change alters their habitat. For instance, as wet grasslands dry up, lapwings are left with few places to breed. Others that prefer warmer conditions, such as Dartford warblers, are taking advantage of milder winters to spread into new areas. New species are even arriving from Europe: little egrets only reached the United Kingdom in the 1980s, but are now common. Meanwhile, summer visitors, such as swallows, are arriving earlier and leaving later. A few, such as the blackcap, are not bothering to leave at all.

Today, the little egret is a common sight in the UK.

The impacts of global warming

You might think that a little climate change sounds like a good thing. After all, wouldn't we all enjoy longer, hotter summers? Well, in some parts of the world there might be a few temporary benefits. However for most people, global warming will have a serious effect on their food, homes, and livelihoods. It may even threaten their lives.

Water worries

One-third of the world's population, close to two billion people, already does not have enough water. Climate change could make things even worse, especially in poorer parts of the world. Drought-prone areas will have even less rainfall, shrinking glaciers will supply less water to rivers, and aquifers (underground water supplies) may dry up. Many densely populated regions will face severe shortages. Half a billion people in India and Bangladesh depend on the Indus and Ganges Rivers, which receive their water from the glaciers of the Himalayas. These glaciers are already melting fast. Elsewhere, rising temperatures will increase the evaporation of water from soil, turning more areas into waterless desert.

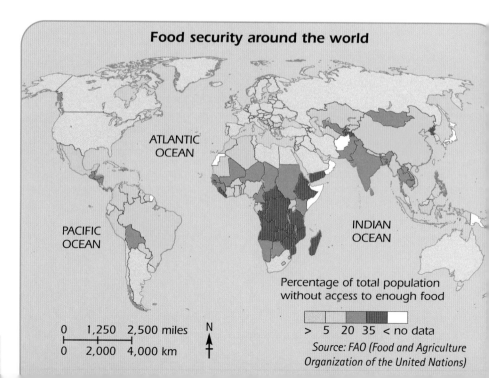

Food security around the world

ATLANTIC OCEAN

PACIFIC OCEAN

INDIAN OCEAN

Percentage of total population without access to enough food

> 5   20   35   < no data

0   1,250   2,500 miles

0   2,000   4,000 km

N

Source: FAO (Food and Agriculture Organization of the United Nations)

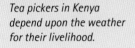

Tea pickers in Kenya depend upon the weather for their livelihood.

Watching the skies

This year, John Karanga is watching the skies nervously. He is a picker on a tea farm in Kenya, where he is paid just enough to support his family. But last year a violent hailstorm destroyed the tea plantation overnight. John had never seen anything like it. With no work left, he had no money to pay school fees, so had to take his children out of school. Kenya depends heavily on growing tea and selling it to other countries. But, as temperatures rise, the soil dries up, rainfall becomes more erratic, and storms destroy crops. If tea farming in Kenya were to fail, the impact on families like John Karanga's would be enormous.

FARMING OR FAMINE?

Farmers depend upon the weather to grow food and feed their animals. However, without enough water they cannot **irrigate** their land. Droughts or violent storms destroy crops, rising sea levels flood coastal farmland, and warmer weather spreads livestock diseases. In **temperate regions**, such as Europe and North America, higher temperatures may produce a longer growing season, allowing farmers to grow more. But at lower latitudes, where most poor countries are, global warming will bring more heat and less water to many areas, making it hard to grow enough food to live.

THE PRICE OF FOOD

At present, there is enough food to feed everyone on the planet but millions still go hungry because they do not have money to buy food, or land on which to grow their own. Politicians agree that food security – which means having access to enough food at all times – should be a basic right for people everywhere. But climate change may already threaten people's food security in poorer countries. Experts predict over 600 million people will go hungry by the year 2060. Many poor countries have to **export** food, to pay their **debts** to richer nations. Meanwhile, the poor nations struggle to grow enough to feed their own people.

People in Kuala Lumpur, Malaysia, wear facemasks to protect against the smog caused by forest fires in nearby Indonesia, 2003.

Falling ill

Climate change can affect our health. The World Health Organization (WHO) estimates that global warming caused at least 150,000 deaths in 2000 alone. Developed countries, which have good public health systems, are mostly managing to cope. However, many developing countries, with fewer resources, are finding it much harder.

TOO HOT TO HANDLE

Hot weather can kill. It is especially dangerous to the very old and the very young, and to people with heart problems, whose hearts must work harder to keep them cool. Heatwaves often hit hardest in cities, where temperatures are higher than in the surrounding countryside. Recent years have seen heatwaves claiming thousands of lives in the United States, India, and Europe.

Holiday horror

At the end of August 2003, the Robin family returned to their Paris apartment after their summer holiday at the seaside. The weather had been blisteringly hot, with record temperatures of over 40°C (104°F) for days on end. They had been able to do little except lie by the pool. The children called their grandmother as soon as they got home; Granny Robin was 83 and lived by herself just round the corner. But she didn't answer her phone. When Mr Robin went round to check on his mother, he found her collapsed in her chair. She had been ill for five days, but there had been nobody to turn to for help and she hadn't managed to get hold of a doctor. Mr Robin rushed his mother to hospital where, after a week, she recovered. She was lucky: 14,802 people died from the searing temperatures in France that summer, many of them elderly and alone.

MALARIA ON THE MARCH

In tropical countries where conditions are warm and wet, mosquitoes and other insects can carry dangerous diseases such as malaria. Malaria kills roughly two million people in Africa every year. Global warming may now be making more places suitable for malaria-carrying mosquitoes. In the highlands of Rwanda, malaria cases have tripled in recent years. Scientists think that if Earth warms by another 2°C (4°F), malaria-carrying mosquitoes may spread to cover 60 per cent of Earth's surface, carrying the disease to many new places.

DIRTY AIR, DIRTY WATER

Global warming may also be helping to pollute our air and water. Higher air temperatures turn air pollution in cities into a harmful smog. This can cause chest pains and breathing difficulties, especially for people with conditions such as asthma (an illness in which a person's air passages become narrower making it hard to breathe). Meanwhile, flooding poses health risks when city **sanitation** services are swamped, spreading unclean water and **sewage**. Dirty water in the tropics can carry dangerous diseases such as cholera. From 1997 to 1998 flooding brought cholera epidemics to several countries along the east coast of Africa, including Somalia, Tanzania, and Mozambique.

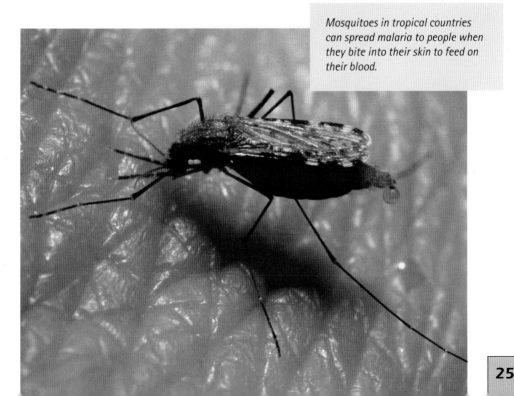

Mosquitoes in tropical countries can spread malaria to people when they bite into their skin to feed on their blood.

Under water

Rising seas destroy beaches, flood cities, contaminate farmland, spread disease, and pollute water supplies. People living on islands and in low-lying coastal regions are most at risk. Unfortunately, over two-thirds of the world's population lives on coastal plains, and eleven of the world's fifteen largest cities are on the coast.

ISLAND CRISIS

Many islands in the Pacific Ocean are at imminent risk. In August 2005, at least 100 villagers on the island of Tegua in the Vanuatu Island group had to move to higher ground. Regular floods had swamped their homes and left coconut palms standing in water.

As flood waters in Bangladesh rose during 2003 it became more difficult for families to collect clean drinking water.

Inhabitants of the nearby Marshall Islands are facing similar problems. Even before their homes become flooded, salt water from the rising seas is seeping into the ground and spoiling their freshwater supply.

FLOODING FARMLAND

Rising sea levels also threaten farmland in river deltas and coastal plains. Sea water seeps through the ground, ruining the soil for crops and making the **water table** too salty for irrigation and drinking. In Bangladesh, an 88 cm (35 in) rise – which is what some scientists predict over the coming century – would flood over half the country's rice farming region. It would also swamp rice farmers in many other populous Asian countries, including India, Thailand, China, Vietnam, and Indonesia.

This coral in Fiji has been "bleached" by warm sea temperatures. If it dies, it can no longer protect the coast from storms.

DEFENCELESS

Natural barriers, such as coral reefs and **mangrove** forests, help to protect many tropical coastlines from the full force of the sea. However, rising sea levels are making conditions too salty for some mangrove trees, while ocean waters are becoming too warm for some coral reefs to survive. Human activities, such as **deforestation** and pollution, are also damaging these habitats, but global warming may be speeding up the process. It was an earthquake, not global warming, that caused the devastating tsunami (tidal wave) that swept the Indian Ocean region on 26 December 2004, killing over 280,000 people. The damage was made worse by the disappearance of natural coastal defences from many of the affected regions.

FUTURE THREATS

Many places face disaster if sea levels keep rising at their present rate. Most of the 1,196 islands that make up the Maldives in the Indian Ocean, for instance, are barely 2 m (7 ft) above sea level, so their 311,000 inhabitants would have nowhere left to go. An even bigger rise would affect the whole world. The collapse of the Western Antarctic Ice Sheet would raise sea levels by 6 m (20 ft), completely flooding London, Florida, Bangkok, Bangladesh, and many other crowded places. Billions of people would be displaced and climate change would make farming impossible in many regions. The good news is that this will probably not happen for at least a thousand years. The bad news is that it will happen one day, and that global warming might speed the process up.

Forced out

As the climate changes the places where we live, it forces many people to move in search of food and shelter. Sometimes, there is nowhere for them to go. At other times, they end up in places that are already struggling, so their arrival makes life harder for everyone.

PACIFIC DEPARTURES

Tuvalu is a tiny island country in the Pacific Ocean. Its highest point is only 5 m (16 ft) above sea level. Rising seas have eroded the coastline, tropical cyclones have battered the islands, and floods have ruined drinking water. In 2002, Tuvalu's 11,000 inhabitants finally abandoned their battle against the sea and set out to find a new home. New Zealand eventually agreed to take them in.

Arctic evictions

Warming is also causing problems for Arctic residents. The Alaskan village of Shishmaref may become the first US community forced to move because of climate change. Erosion at this remote Arctic settlement has moved at 4–7 m (13–23 ft) per year since 2001, over three times the previous rate. Melting sea ice has allowed violent storms to eat away at the island, while buildings are starting to slump as the ground thaws. In 2005, the village's 600 residents decided to move to a more solid site 22 km (14 miles) inland. The cost of their move was estimated at £82–100 million (US$150–180 million).

This house in Alaska collapsed when the frozen ground started to thaw.

DESERT WANDERERS

The Sahel region of northwest Africa has suffered severe droughts since the 1970s. Poor and unpredictable rainfall, which some scientists have blamed on global warming, has helped turn many areas into desert. Millions of people have fled their homes just to survive. In 2004, drought hit the country of Niger, leaving 2.5 million people without enough food. Cattle herders who had lost their livestock moved to farming areas, where they found that a locust invasion had destroyed 15 per cent of crops. Many people left the countryside, ending up in city slums or fleeing to neighbouring countries such as Ghana, Nigeria, and Benin.

FINDING SPACE

More and more people will soon be on the move as global warming brings further changes to our environment. Human migration is set to become one of the biggest challenges for humanity in the 21st century. People in secure parts of the world will have to share their space and resources with those whose homes are no longer fit for living in.

WHAT DO YOU THINK?
Our country is too crowded to take in any more refugees

- Some people are worried about increasing immigration. They fear that their country will not be able to cope with all the extra people.
- Others think that wealthy countries should help poorer ones. Climate change is a global problem so we must all learn to share.

Many people who look for a better place to live end up in overcrowded city slums, where they have to fight poverty and disease.

Wildlife in danger

Some wildlife is heading for **extinction** as global warming affects the balance of nature. When one animal or plant disappears, it often causes knock-on effects for others.

POLAR PERILS

Polar bears are in trouble. These big Arctic predators use floating sea ice to get around in search of ringed seals, their favourite prey. With the ice melting earlier in spring, the seals are drifting out of reach just when female polar bears need extra food for their young cubs. When the ice freezes late in autumn, hungry bears cannot reach their winter feeding-grounds in time. Some have taken to raiding rubbish dumps in Arctic towns, such as Churchill in Canada.

Meanwhile, shrinking sea ice in the Southern Ocean means there is less of the marine algae that grows underneath it. Less algae means fewer of the shrimp-like creatures called krill that are the staple diet of Adelie penguins. Adelie penguins once bred in huge colonies on the Antarctic Peninsula. Most have now disappeared.

This polar bear searches for a snack on a burning rubbish dump in Churchill, Canada. Its usual food, seals, lies out of reach across the sea.

Vanishing toad

The golden toad may be the first species to have been driven to extinction by climate change. This brilliantly coloured amphibian inhabited an area of **cloud forest** in Costa Rica in Central America, where a constant cloak of mist once provided the perfect damp conditions for breeding. However, the recent warming of the surrounding oceans has caused the mist to form higher up the mountains than before. This robbed the toads of their habitat, and also left them more vulnerable to deadly skin diseases and direct heat from the sun. Nobody has seen a golden toad since 1989.

We will never again see golden toads gathering to breed. This colouful little animal may now be extinct.

CORAL CRASH

In recent years, a condition called "bleaching" – when coral turns white and can die – has attacked coral reefs all over the world. In 2002, it devastated much of Australia's Great Barrier Reef. Coral gets its colour from microscopic plants called zooxanthellae. They live inside coral and provide it with food. Bleaching occurs when warmer temperatures than usual drive out the zooxanthellae. A rise of just 1°C (3°F) above normal can cause this to happen. Coral reefs provide a nursery for thousands of fish species, which are left homeless when the coral disappears.

INVASIONS

Animals moving into new areas can cause big problems. In Canada, for instance, the mountain pine beetle is taking advantage of milder winters to head northwards. This beetle can infest elderly or damaged trees. In British Columbia alone, it affected 70,000 km² (27,000 sq miles) of forest in 2004, killing millions of trees. Hot dry summers make trees more susceptible to beetle attack, and dead trees, in turn, become more susceptible to forest fires. So, the beetle is helping to destroy whole forests, which leaves many other plants and animals without a home.

Taking action

What can we do about global warming and climate change? Both governments and individuals have a part to play.

DIFFERENT VIEWS

Not everybody agrees about climate change. Many scientists believe that people are causing global warming and that to stop it we must change the way in which we live, especially by using less fossil fuel. Others think that global warming is a natural process and that there is no point making difficult changes to our way of life. The **United Nations** (UN) set up the Intergovernmental Panel on Climate Change (IPCC) to look into the issue. In 2001, it concluded that: "There is new and stronger evidence that most of the warming observed over the last 50 years is attributable to human activities." This has convinced most governments to take action.

SETTING TARGETS

In 2002, members of the UN signed an agreement in the Japanese city of Kyoto, called the Kyoto Protocol. This obliged them to reduce greenhouse gas emissions (the amount of greenhouse gases they release into the atmosphere) by the year 2010. Each country was set a different target, according to its needs. The United Kingdom, for instance, agreed to reduce emissions by 9 per cent below its 1990 levels. The Kyoto Protocol stated that if countries failed to reach their targets, they would have to pay for any extra carbon they used.

As cities like Shanghai in China continue to grow, the problem of global warming looks set to increase.

Protestors at a meeting in Sydney, Australia, urge their governments to find alternatives to fossil fuels.

BEYOND KYOTO

Not everybody was happy with the Kyoto Protocol. Some countries – including the United States, Australia, and China – refused to sign, arguing that they could not afford to meet their targets. Poor countries felt that reducing their emissions would prevent them from developing. Environmental groups, meanwhile, thought the targets did not go far enough. They wanted countries to reduce emissions by at least 20 per cent by 2010, and by 60 per cent by 2050. They argued that this was the only way to secure our planet for future generations.

In December 2005, the UN had another meeting to discuss climate change, this time in Montreal, Canada. Now, more people were in agreement about the Kyoto targets. Wealthier nations agreed to help poorer nations meet their targets in a way that did not prevent development. The United States also agreed to take action. It seemed that the world had begun to take climate change more seriously.

BOTTOM DOLLAR

Money is at the heart of disagreements about how to tackle global warming. Some fear that cutting fossil fuels would restrict industry and business, making their countries poorer. Others point out that allowing global warming to increase would prove far more costly, since it would damage every part of the community. Today, **carbon offset schemes** allow businesses and others to offset (balance) their consumption of fossil fuels by making payments towards energy-saving projects.

Choosing energy

Experts predict that we will use 59 per cent more energy in 2020 than we did in 1999. Using it wisely will be the key to tackling climate change. There are two main kinds of energy: renewable, such as solar power, that we can use again and again; and non-renewable, such as oil, that we use up and cannot replace. Most energy today is non-renewable. It produces the CO_2 and other greenhouse gases that help cause global warming.

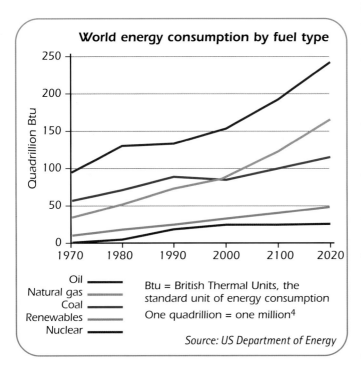

World energy consumption by fuel type

Quadrillion Btu

Oil
Natural gas
Coal
Renewables
Nuclear

Btu = British Thermal Units, the standard unit of energy consumption

One quadrillion = one million[4]

Source: US Department of Energy

OILING THE WHEELS

For decades, the developed world has relied on oil. Countries such as Saudi Arabia or Venezuela depend upon producing and selling it. Other nations need it to power their electricity, industry, and transport. This means the oil industry is very rich and powerful. In 2005, the Exxon Mobil oil company made a profit of £5.4 billion (US$9.92 billion) in just three months. That's more money than the large African country of Tanzania makes in a year. Governments help out the oil industry and in turn the oil industry supports these governments.

ENERGY SAVING

Fossil fuels would go further if we made a few simple changes. We would save energy and reduce greenhouse gas emissions by using more public transport instead of cars and by using less electricity in our homes and businesses. We could also use more efficient fossil fuels, such as natural gas, which produces less CO_2 than coal or oil.

A man in Sudan cleans solar panels that help provide his village with renewable energy from the Sun.

CLEAN ENERGY

Alternatively, we could switch to using renewable energy sources, such as wind, solar or hydroelectric power. These are known as "clean energy", since they generate power without emitting greenhouse gases. They are also renewable, which means we can use them again and again. Today, only about 9 per cent of the world's energy comes from renewable sources. Most is in the developing world, where at least two billion people (one-third of Earth's population) have no electricity. But we should be able to use far more of it everywhere. Wind power alone could meet one-fifth of US electricity needs. The Kyoto Protocol now encourages governments to invest in developing renewable energy.

THE NUCLEAR OPTION

Nuclear power offers another alternative to fossil fuels. It uses a metal called uranium to produce lots of energy from small amounts of fuel. Although it is not renewable, it does not produce harmful amounts of greenhouse gases. Nuclear power provides around 11 per cent of the world's energy needs. However, some people think it is not the answer. Nuclear waste is very dangerous, because it is **radioactive**, which means it can cause cancer and other diseases. It remains radioactive for thousands of years. Disposing of the waste safely is risky: an accident could cause a major disaster.

Workers in Sri Lanka build a new house for a family whose home was destroyed by floods.

For richer or for poorer

Developing countries suffer more from climate change than wealthy ones do. They are less able to protect themselves against disasters such as drought, famine, and disease. Many people live in flimsy houses and on poor land that is more at risk from problems such as flooding. They rely on growing their own food. When disaster strikes, their governments may not have the money or resources to help them out.

World energy consumption relative to population

Country	% of energy consumed	% of world population
United States	25.0	4.6
China	9.9	21.2
Russia	7.0	2.5
Japan	5.8	2.1
Germany	3.9	1.3
India	3.1	16.6
France	2.9	0.9
UK	2.6	1.0
Canada	2.5	0.5
South Korea	1.9	0.7

Source: US Department of Energy

INJUSTICE

Rich nations are contributing much more to global warming: they burn more fossil fuel and produce more CO_2. The average person in the United States, for instance, uses about 15 times more energy than the average person in the developing world. Australians produce 34 times more CO_2 emissions per person on average than their poorer neighbours on the Tuvalu Islands. Yet it is the Tuvalu islanders who have had to abandon their homes as sea levels continue to rise.

THE RIGHT TO DEVELOP

Poor countries would like to develop and enjoy all the advantages of wealthy, **industrialized nations**. But the wealthy nations, worried that this will increase global warming, want to restrict them. Poor countries think this is unfair. They argue, understandably, that global warming is not their fault and that they have every right to develop. Many are reluctant to agree to CO_2 reduction plans. The developing world is now set to overtake the developed world as the main producer of CO_2 by 2010.

DIFFERENT TARGETS

The Kyoto Protocol recognizes that rich nations must help poor ones to develop in a way that doesn't increase global warming. But giving money is not enough: money or even food aid will be useless if climate change becomes worse. Instead, rich countries must provide technology and skills, so that poor countries can meet their rising energy demands without damaging their environment and climate. But rich countries must also lead by example, reducing their own carbon emissions and developing alternatives to fossil fuels.

WHAT DO YOU THINK? More cars for China?

- China has a population of 1.3 billion people and is developing fast. Today, more Chinese people want cars.
- Americans are worried that traffic pollution in China will cause serious damage to the world's climate.
- About one in every two Americans owns a car. In China, only about one in 140 has one.
- Why shouldn't Chinese people enjoy the same things as Americans?

TAKING RESPONSIBILITY

Some people believe that climate change links poverty in the developing world to the comfortable lifestyles of people in the developed world. A drought in Africa, for instance, may be due to global warming that much wealthier nations have helped cause. If this is true, then perhaps wealthy nations have a duty to help poorer ones. Anyway, sooner or later, climate change will affect everyone – rich or poor. So it is in everybody's interests to tackle the problem together.

People all over Africa, such as these women in Kenya, still rely upon farming to survive. Climate change may spell disaster for them.

Activists from the environmental group Greenpeace protest against global warming at a power plant in the Philippines.

Making a difference

Governments are battling climate change, but there are also many simple ways in which we can all help reduce global warming.

One-tonne Challenge

Canada is the world's third highest polluter per head of population: the average Canadian produces more than 5 tonnes of greenhouse gases a year. The Canadian government has set up the "One-tonne challenge". It asks every Canadian to reduce their greenhouse gas emissions by one tonne per year. A free information pack provides helpful tips on how to save energy, conserve resources, and reduce waste. It also shows people how to calculate how much carbon they use in their everyday lives.

HOME SAVINGS

Over one-quarter of CO_2 emissions in most developed countries come from the home. We can all help to save energy by turning off lights and appliances when we are not using them. It costs a lot of energy to supply, treat, and heat water, so we should also use that carefully. Cars produce nearly half the greenhouse gas emissions for many families, so we should try to use them less. Aircraft are even worse polluters: one return flight from London to New York produces about 4 tonnes (4.4 tons) of CO_2 per person – the same as an average car produces in a year. By flying less we would make a huge difference.

WHY BOTHER?

You might think there's no point trying to save energy at home when big polluters, such as airlines and oil companies, continue to pump CO_2 into the atmosphere. But small changes have a big impact if enough people make them. For instance, if everybody in the United Kingdom turned off their televisions instead of leaving them on standby overnight, they would stop half a million tonnes of CO_2 being released into the atmosphere. If every American home replaced their standard light bulbs with energy efficient ones, together they would save as much in greenhouse gas emissions as eight million cars produce each year.

Ten top tips – simple ways to save energy:

1. **Recycle waste:** glass, cans, paper, and cardboard all cost energy to produce.
2. **Compost food waste:** use it in your garden.
3. **Switch to renewable energy:** this could save your home over a tonne of CO_2 per year.
4. **Save water:** fit low-flow showerheads and a low-flush toilet; only use the dishwasher when full.
5. **Buy locally produced food:** most supermarket food has travelled a long way, causing pollution.
6. **Turn off lights:** also fit energy-efficient bulbs for those you use most.
7. **Insulate your home:** seal gaps and cracks to save energy and lower your heating bill.
8. **Leave the car at home:** share someone else's car, take a bus, cycle, or walk.
9. **Holiday at home:** don't fly unless you have to.
10. **Grow your own food:** saves energy, packaging, and waste.

Cycling is a simple way of getting around that saves energy. It also helps you to get fit!

Future climate

We cannot know exactly what to expect from climate change in ten years' time, let alone a hundred. But we do know that life will be different for many people.

ENERGY ADJUSTMENTS

Our appetite for energy is not slowing down. Experts expect us to use 60 per cent more energy by 2020, with CO_2 emissions rising at 3–7 per cent per year. Yet oil reserves will not last forever. Some experts think they will start to decline from 2007, so people will have to find new energy sources. We may be using twice as much natural gas by 2020, while wind and solar power could be supplying nearly half the world's electricity.

MOVING AROUND

As the world changes, people will have to move. Some will head for higher ground as low-lying areas become flooded. In the United Kingdom, for instance, many areas around London may become uninhabitable. Those in poorer regions will be hit harder. By 2050, Africa is set to suffer a 10 per cent drop in rainfall, a 1.6°C (3°F) rise in temperature and, at worst, a 25 cm (9 in) rise in sea level.

This ecological village in Denmark has solar power and many other energy-saving features that show how people may be able to live in the future.

This will cause food and water shortages that force millions of people to move. Many will head for cities, creating more overcrowding and yet more demand for fuel. Others will head for richer countries, where resources may become stretched. Already, 12 million people in China are leaving the countryside every year. The government plans to build hundreds of new cities in order to house them.

HELP FROM MACHINES

Technology will help us adapt to climate change. New machinery will use renewable energy sources – such as hydrogen cell vehicles, which generate electricity for engine power using a chemical reaction between oxygen and hydrogen. Future governments will have to invest more money in developing "clean"

This hydrogen-fuelled vehicle is one example of how new technology can make use of renewable energy.

technology, making it cheaper, more efficient, and available to everyone.

SAVING AND SHARING

In developed parts of the world, such as Europe and North America, climate change may alter the way people live. Instead of simply buying and using up energy and resources, we will learn to save and recycle as much as possible within the home. We may also learn to share things within our communities, such as transport, so that we generate less waste.

AN UNCERTAIN FUTURE

By the end of the 21st century, the world may be a very different place. The polar sea ice may all have melted, allowing ships to travel from Europe to Japan via the North Pole. The tropical forests may all have been burned or cut down, yet tropical plants and diseases may have spread to Europe and North America. Climate changes will affect us all in one way or another: where we live, what we eat, how we get around. The effects of climate in the future may depend upon what we are doing now. The future starts today.

Statistical information

Selected CO$_2$ emissions by country per capita (person) in 2000

	metric tonnes	tons		metric tonnes	tons
Qatar	70.1	77.2	Ukraine	6.0	6.6
United States	20.6	22.7	Iran	4.7	5.1
Canada	18.7	20.6	Chile	3.9	4.2
Australia	18.2	20.0	Iraq	3.3	3.6
Saudi Arabia	16.9	18.6	Turkey	3.2	3.5
Singapore	14.7	16.2	Seychelles	2.9	3.1
Faroe Islands	14.2	15.6	China	2.2	2.4
Czech Republic	12.5	13.7	Brazil	1.8	1.9
Belgium	12.3	13.5	Maldives	1.7	1.8
Ireland	11.6	12.7	Zimbabwe	1.2	1.3
Libya	10.9	12.0	India	1.1	1.2
Israel	10.5	11.5	Philippines	1.0	1.1
Germany	10.4	11.4	Pakistan	0.7	0.8
Russia	10.0	11.0	Sri Lanka	0.5	0.6
Japan	9.8	10.8	Vanuatu	0.4	0.4
United Kingdom	9.3	10.2	Kenya	0.3	0.3
South Korea	9.1	10.0	Nigeria	0.3	0.3
New Zealand	8.1	8.9	Bangladesh	0.2	0.2
Italy	8.0	8.8	Nepal	0.1	0.1
South Africa	7.4	8.1	Tanzania	0.1	0.1
Venezuela	6.5	7.1	Chad	0.0	0.0
Portugal	6.3	6.9	(World average	3.9	4.2)

Source: United Nations Statistics Division

Malaria statistics

- 300–500 million clinical cases of malaria worldwide each year
- 1.5–2.7 million deaths worldwide from malaria each year
- 50% of deaths of African children under five due to malaria
- 2,800 children per day die of malaria in Africa alone
- 40% of the world's population (2 billion people) at risk of malaria
- 80–90% of malaria deaths occur in sub-Saharan Africa
- 275 million people in sub-Saharan Africa estimated to carry malaria parasites in their blood

Source: World Health Organization

Top 21 countries by CO₂ emissions in 2002 (each above 1% of total)

Country	Metric tonnes	Tons	% of total
World total	24,126,416	26,594,82	100%
United States	5,872,278	6,473,078	24.3
China (PRC)	3,550,371	3,913,614	14.5
Russia	1,432,513	1,579,075	5.9
India	1,220,926	1,345,840	5.1
Japan	1,203,535	1,326,671	5.0
Germany	804,701	887,031	3.3
United Kingdom	544,813	600,553	2.3
Canada	517,157	570,068	2.1
South Korea	446,190	491,840	1.8
Italy	433,018	477,320	1.8
Mexico	383,671	422,924	1.6
France	378,267	416,967	1.6
Iran	360,223	397,077	1.5
Australia	356,342	392,799	1.5
South Africa	345,382	380,723	1.4
Saudi Arabia	340,555	375,397	1.4
Brazil	313,757	345,857	1.3
Ukraine	306,807	338,196	1.3
Indonesia	306,491	337,848	1.3
Spain	304,603	335,767	1.3
Poland	296,398	326,722	1.2

Source: United Nations Statistics Division

Ten most expensive Atlantic hurricanes
(cost of damage in millions of US$)

Name	Year	Damage
Katrina	2005	80,000
Andrew	1992	26,500
Charley	2004	15,000
Wilma	2005	14,400
Ivan	2004	14,200
Rita	2005	9,400
Frances	2004	8,900
Hugo	1989	7,000
Jeanne	2004	6,900
Allison*	2001	5,000

* tropical storm

Source: US National Hurricane Center

Kyoto Protocol targets

This table shows targets recommended by the Kyoto Protocol, by which selected countries should reduce their greenhouse gas emissions. The figures represent changes relative to 1990 emissions. A negative figure means the country should reduce its emissions below 1990 levels. A positive figure means the country may continue to increase its emissions, but the rate of increase will be slower than at present.

Austria	-13.0%
Belgium	-7.5%
Denmark	-21.0%
Germany	-21.0%
Italy	-6.5%
Netherlands	-6.0%
United Kingdom	-12.5%
(EU average	-8.0%)
Canada	-8.0%
Japan	-6.0%
United States	-7.0%
Russian Federation	0.0%
Australia	+8.0%
Iceland	+12%

Source: DTI (UK Department of Trade and Industry)

Glossary

atmosphere blanket of gases that surrounds Earth. It includes the air we breathe.

carbon offset scheme arrangement that allows an organization to pay for its CO_2 emissions by contributing to energy conservation, for example, by planting trees

cloud forest type of tropical forest in hilly regions with constant mist

debt money owed by one person, or one country, to another

deciduous trees that shed their leaves in cold or dry seasons in order to conserve water. They are found in temperate regions.

deforestation cutting down forests, usually to provide timber or to clear land for farming

density mass of a substance per unit volume

developed country (developed world) nation, such as the United States or Australia, with a relatively high standard of living due to its advanced economy

developing country (developing world) nation, such as Kenya or India, where most people rely upon farming and are poorer than those in developed nations

erosion gradual changing of land by natural processes, such as the action of sea, wind, or ice

evaporate when water heats up and turns into a gas, called water vapour. Steam and clouds are water vapour.

export sell goods to another country

extinction when an animal or plant species dies out completely

glacier mass of ice that flows slowly downhill towards the coast

habitat particular place where an animal or plant lives, such as a desert or forest

hibernation deep sleep lasting several months that helps some animals to survive winter

hurricane powerful, rotating storm with wind speeds of 100 kilometres (62 miles) per hour or more (called a cyclone in the Indian Ocean and a typhoon in the Pacific)

ice age prehistoric period when ice sheets covered much of Earth. The last ice age ended about 12,000 years ago.

Industrial Revolution period of European history from the late 18th century when the invention of industrial machinery changed society

industrialized nation nation, usually developed, whose economy relies upon industry and manufacturing

irrigate to supply water to fields for growing crops

landfill site site for disposing of domestic or industrial waste – usually in a tip or underground

latitude measurement of distance from the Equator: a low latitude is close to the Equator; a high latitude is close to the Poles

mangrove type of tree that grows in shallow salt water on tropical coasts

marmot animal like a squirrel that lives in mountain regions

orbit regular circular journey made by objects in space, such as Earth's circuit around the Sun

photosynthesis process by which plants produce food. They use sunlight to combine carbon dioxide with water in a chemical reaction.

plankton microscopic animals and plants that float in water

polar regions areas within the Arctic and Antarctic circles that surround, respectively, the North and South Poles

radioactivity release of energy called radiation from inside atoms; radiation is harmful to all living things

sanitation safe collection and disposal of sewage and other waste from houses

sewage water containing human waste

smog fog of thick polluting smoke in cities

spawning when animals such as frogs and fish lay their eggs

temperate regions areas of Earth that lie between the Poles and the tropics

tropics area of Earth either side of the Equator, between the Tropic of Cancer and the Tropic of Capricorn

tundra land within the Arctic Circle where the ice melts in summer and small plants grow

United Nations (UN) international organization comprising most nations of the world, in which these nations make decisions together

water table water lying permanently underground

water vapour gas that forms when water heats up and enters the atmosphere

Further information

Burnie, David. *Earth Watch* (Dorling Kindersley, 2001)
This book provides an overview of the many serious problems that our planet faces at the start of the 21st century, including climate change.

Oxlade, Chris. *Global Warming* (Bridgestone Books/Capstone Press, 2003)
This book explores the complex issue of climate change, discussing both the causes and effects. It includes related science activities and suggestions for ways to help slow global warming.

Rogers, Kirsteen. *The Usborne Internet-Linked Introduction to Weather and Climate Change* (Usborne Publishing Ltd, 2003)
This book has clear explanations on all aspects of climate change, with links to recommended websites and downloadable images.

Silverstein, Alvin, et al. *Global Warming* (Twenty-First Century Books/ Millbrook Press, 2003)
In this book, find out about the different periods of weather through history and learn how we can help slow the effects of global warming today.

FOR OLDER READERS

Fagan, Brian. *The Long Summer: How Climate Changed Civilization* (Granta Books, 2005)
This book tells how human history has always been influenced by the changing climate, providing a historical context in which to understand global warming today. Adult help required.

Websites

The UK Department of the Environment
www.defra.gov.uk/schools
Lots of information about climate change, with information and activities for schools and children.

The Environmental Protection Agency
www.epa.gov/globalwarming/kids
Information about climate change and global warming, with games and activities for children.

Climate Hot Map.org
www.climatehotmap.org
A website that maps the effects of climate change around the globe using interesting examples and case studies. Compiled by the World Wildlife Fund, the Union of Concerned Scientists, and others.

The BBC Weather Centre
www.bbc.co.uk/climate
This website has all the latest news stories related to climate change around the world.

GreenLiving.co.uk
www.greenliving.co.uk
A website with lots of useful tips on saving energy around your home and helping to reduce your carbon footprint.

Contact addresses

US Department of Energy
1000 Independence Ave., SW
Washington, DC 20585, USA
Tel: (+1) 800-dial-DOE
www.energy.gov/index.htm

DEFRA
(UK Dept of the Environment)
Information Resource Centre
Lower Ground Floor
Ergon House, c/o Nobel House
17 Smith Square
London SW1P 3JR, UK
Tel: (+44) 08459 33 55 77
www.defra.gov.uk

Friends of the Earth International
PO Box 19199, 1000 GD Amsterdam,
The Netherlands
Tel: (+31) 20 622 1369
www.foei.org/index.php

Greenpeace International
Ottho Heldringstraat 5
1066 AZ Amsterdam
The Netherlands
Tel: (+31) 20 7182000
www.greenpeace.org

WWF
Panda House, Weyside Park
Godalming, Surrey GU7 1XR, UK
Tel: (+44) 01483 426444
www.wwf.org

Earth Policy Institute
1350 Connecticut Ave., NW
Washington, DC 20036, USA
Tel: (+1) 202 496 9290
www.earth-policy.org

Index

Titles in the *Planet Under Pressure* series include:

PLANET UNDER PRESSURE
WATER
LOUISE AND RICHARD SPILSBURY

Hardback   1 4062 0534 6

PLANET UNDER PRESSURE
HEALTH AND DISEASE
CLAIRE WALLERSTEIN

Hardback   1 4062 0535 4

PLANET UNDER PRESSURE
ANIMALS UNDER THREAT
LOUISE AND RICHARD SPILSBURY

Hardback   1 4062 0537 0

PLANET UNDER PRESSURE
CLIMATE CHANGE
MIKE UNWIN

Hardback   1 4062 0536 2

Find out about other titles from Heinemann Library on our website www.heinemann.co.uk/library